CLASSROOM CHUCKLES

Bill Knowlton

SCHOLASTIC BOOK SERVICES

NEW YORK·TORONTO·LONDON·AUCKLAND·SYDNEY·TOKYO

ISBN: 0-590-08027-X

19 18 17 16 15 14 13 12 11 10 9   0 1 2 3 4/8

Printed in the U.S.A   06

FOR TEACHERS ONLY

I would like to dedicate this book to those teachers who teach with a determination to make children stretch to become *more* than they are but, at the same time, take the time to enjoy them for *what* they are — refreshing, unpredictable, and sometimes very funny people. Your ability to laugh with these young people is an immutable requirement for good teaching — and may even mean your survival in the classroom.

Bill Knowlton

"Who's in charge here?"

"I've heard of trade schools,
and I'd like to!"

"He has trouble seeing the blackboard!"

"We did *that* last year — how come we have to do it again this year?"

"I'm an underachiever....
What's your racket?"

9

"The only answers I knew today were for the
toothpaste test."

"One of them was bound to call you 'our senior citizen' sooner or later."

"I take it that I am correct then, in numbering you among my critics."

"Back again, Master Biggs?"

"My brain's all aching and racked with pain!"

"You mean we have to process all that data?"

"It figures."

"Come now, Miss Twist,
your class isn't *that* large!"

"...then she said, 'There's a place for everything
and everything in its place'...
and she sent me in here!"

18

"He means arithmetic, not atomic."

"I don't know...maybe his name is Reason...
he's always saying listen to it!"

"If it's true that in this country anyone can grow
up to be President, I'm worried!"

"The proliferation of knowledge has reached a
rate too fast for me to cope with!"

"Here's one book you can
judge by the cover!"

"After looking around he's decided he doesn't
want to prepare to take over
when his time comes!"

"He's the only person I've ever known who has become a legend in his own lifetime!"

"His mother's right . . . He *does* have
an inquiring mind!"

"Dick! Come back here this minute!"

"You just mentioned my weakest subject —
school!"

"...but, how high is *up* in *light years*?"

"Master Biggs, may I have a few anxious moments of your time?"

"Maybe he's trying to tell us something!"

"I've just lost my will to live!"

"She's got it backwards....The rest of the class
doesn't cooperate with *me*!"

"Give it to me straight. Have I got the goods or haven't I?"

"We're so happy you could stop in and observe
our unit on the American Indian, Mr. Milby."

"He wants to sit in the back of the room."

"It's a letter of resignation!"

"They *sound* all right to me."

"Of course you realize you have completely
undermined my confidence!"

"I didn't learn anything in history class....All anybody learns from history is that we never learn from history."

41

"I say he's a wiggler. He says he's doing his iso-
metric exercises!"

"When's pay day?"

"I agree with what you say, Charlie, but I'm not
going to help you defend your right to say it!"

"There's one thing I want to make clear — I will *not* be influenced by a pressure group."

"I wish they'd quit working on a machine to
replace teachers and invent one
to replace students!"

"...and suddenly there were teachers
all over the place!"

"It's for you!"

"He could be a good student if he weren't so careless."

49

"It looks like *everyone* is at his battle station this morning."

"When they programed Miss Twist they threw away the tape!"

"I like your perfume, Miss Twist — it smells like peanut butter."

"There are *some* changes in education that I don't try to keep up with!"

"Why don't you do something to get sent in there?
He has the World Series on television!"

"...and during our study of the Westward Movement he cheers for the Indians!"

"You gotta admit—he really tries!"

"Congratulations, Dimbleby — this is the *earliest*
you've been *tardy* all week!"

"When can you start?"

"Sort of shakes you, doesn't it?"

"He didn't make one...says he's not going to be fingerprinted!"

"We shared something a little
different today."

"What's so terrible about fighting?...Alexander
the Great, Caesar, Napoleon, and General Grant
did all right doing it!"

"While the rest of society worries about the drop-
out problem I have a couple of drop-ins
to upset me!"

"You mean you want me to confess without my having been informed of my right to counsel?"

"A word of warning, Mr. Milby. . . . Don't let the teacher catch you cheating on those addition problems!"

"Little Miss Muffet sat on her tuffet
eating her vitamin-enriched curds and whey.
Along came a..."

67

"Did *you* invite them?"

"Nothing succeeds like *recess!*"

"Any questions?"

"Frankly, I never thought she'd blow the whistle
on me!"

"Why don't you stay and hear the 9:30 a.m. local news report?"

"The Student Council just voted to do away with
your job!"

"I'm not a satisfied customer!"

"Of course you can't read it.
It's written in a secret code."

"The only thing I learned today was the teacher's boiling point."

"One question...Who makes *you* behave?"

"I've just been informed that I might be replaced by a machine."

"He says all he *has* to tell me is his name, grade, and locker number!"

"If he meant what I think he meant, I'm glad I
didn't understand it!"

"Can I help it if my mind wanders?"

"It was the *largest* paperwad I've ever seen!"

"Does the school psychologist know you harbor
this hidden hostility toward me?"

"The teacher and my mother are in there having a good cry."

"I don't think changing his teaching machine
because it doesn't understand him
will help, Mrs. Milsap."

"How do you expect me to remember what I learned yesterday, Miss...er... what's your name again?"

"Sometimes I think the human race already knows too much for its own good ... and *that's* why I didn't do my homework!"

"I had thought I didn't like school, until he just
explained to me that I do."

"She certainly has me pegged—hasn't she?"

"Abraham Lincoln wasn't right — you can't fool
some of the people *any* of the time!"

"What! No trading stamps?"

"It's one of my better sales talks on reasons for completing homework on time!"

"Remember, sometimes misbehavior is in the eye of the beholder."

"I'll never understand arithmetic if I live to be twelve!"

"Wait a minute until I run it through
my computer."

"After all, *anybody* can be right
if he's the principal!"